FOOTBALL HEROES

RBWM

LIBRARY

SERVICES

by **Anthony Masters**

Illustrated by Ian Heard

W
FRANKLIN WATTS
LONDON•SYDNEY

Editor-in-Chief John C. Miles
Designer Jason Billin/Billin Design Solutions
Art Director Jonathan Hair

Cover artwork by Mark Bergin

First published in 2000
by Franklin Watts
96 Leonard Street
London
EC2A 4XD

Franklin Watts Australia
56 O'Riordan Street
Alexandria
NSW 2015

ISBN 0 7496 3722 6 (hbk)
        0 7496 4005 7 (pbk)

Dewey classification: 796.334

A CIP catalogue record for this book is available
from the British Library.

Printed in Great Britain

CONTENTS

GARY LINEKER

■ CHAPTER ONE

It was unbelievable, as unreal as a dream. But in Gary Lineker's case it was a dream come true. In one season of schoolboy football, he scored an amazing total of 160 goals. Lineker went on to become one of the outstanding players of his generation.

Always honest, he knew he never had the natural gifts of Glen Hoddle or Paul Gascoigne.
'I was more of a deliberate and methodical player who had to work

hard at his craft,' he admitted.
Yet by the summer of 1985, Gary
Lineker was the hottest property in
British football.

How did he do it?

By mastering the tactics of the game
– and practising very hard.
Lineker always thought carefully about
what he was doing and slowly but
surely perfected his game.

Tactics were Lineker's speciality
and he started to learn, practise and
use them in his early teens. His
parents recognised his aims and
encouraged their determined son all
the way.

Eventually Lineker was spotted by
a Leicester City scout who invited
him to train twice a week at the club.
There he was coached by George
Lewis, the Youth Team coach and a

former striker for Leicester City.

Lineker remembers, 'George was the perfect coach for a young striker. He devised training sessions for attacking players which invariably involved different kinds of finishing, be it crossing, shooting or heading, from every angle.'

As a result of such brilliant coaching, as well as his own hard work, Lineker turned professional at the age of 18. Then he was given his Second Division chance by Leicester manager Jock Wallace in a game against Oldham on New Year's Day 1979.

■ CHAPTER TWO

Three months later, Lineker scored his first league goal. Despite such a good beginning, however, he was still seen by management as a fairly ordinary player.

But Gary Lineker had two very good ideas. First, he knew he had to make his game and career the most important things in his life. Second, he had to stand back after each game and take a careful look at every tactic he had tried to use – and whether it had worked out well or not.

This concentration on his game paid off. In 1982-83, Lineker became the Second Division's top scorer with 26 goals. Leicester then returned to the First Division.

By 1984, Lineker's hard work and cool study of his own play was bringing him more and more success. He was becoming seen as the most exciting young striker in the UK.

Then came a transfer – and with it a sum of money that immediately made headlines.

After a lot of bargaining, Everton offered £800,000 for Lineker.

But he still had the difficult task of replacing Andy Gray.

Lineker remembers, 'I knew he was

going to be a tough act to follow. I scored in my first game for Everton against Spurs. I then got a hat-trick against Birmingham at home.'

It wasn't until after Christmas, when Lineker scored against Manchester United and later got two goals against Sheffield Wednesday, that he felt the fans were really supporting him.

Lineker's main aim was to live up to his own high standards.

CHAPTER THREE

Lineker ended the 1984-85 season as the First Division's top scorer with over thirty goals in the net.

He was able to think on his feet. The tense final against Liverpool was a case in point.

The ball had been passed to Lineker deep in the Everton half.

As he raced towards the Liverpool goal, he knew that he had to keep calm, remember his planned tactics and keep his mind on what he was doing. What was more, all this had to be done at high speed.

As a player from the opposing team ran towards him, he knew that the only way through to the goal-mouth was to run faster than he was. Gary Lineker put on a last-minute spurt.

Bruce Grobbelaar, the Liverpool goalkeeper, stopped Lineker's first shot, but he followed through to score the goal.

Sadly for Everton, Liverpool scored three goals in the second half and won the game.

Lineker never claimed glory for himself. Instead, he looked carefully at how Everton worked as a team. Talking about his strike-partner, Graeme Sharp, he said, 'We worked hard to develop our understanding and we seemed to improve with each game.'

Sharp had a great first touch and was brilliant in the air. As a result, Lineker received a large number of 'flick-ons' from him. 'Graeme got over twenty goals himself that season,' he remembers.

In February 1986 Lineker was voted Players' Player of the Year by the PFA. He was also invited to the dinner which was to be held at the Grosvenor House Hotel in London's Park Lane on Sunday March 23rd.

This invitation was to become as tense as any close-run match.

The problem was that Lineker was supposed to be in the USSR with the English squad, training for a friendly match. But there had been problems with the squad's travel arrangements and the team wouldn't know whether they would be going or not until Friday March 21st.

If the game was called off then Lineker would be able to go to the dinner and receive the greatest honour of his career. If the game went ahead, then something else would have to be done about the award.

In the end, a pre-recording of Lineker receiving the award was made. This could then be shown at the dinner if he wasn't able to be there himself.

It was also decided that, if necessary Howard Kendall, the Everton boss, would present the PFA trophy to Lineker at a surprise lunch at their home ground, Goodison Park, after the Friday training session.

The Player of the Year trophy was handed to Eric Woodward in Manchester. Depending on whether the friendly against the USSR was on or off, Woodward planned to take the trophy either to London for the national presentation, or to the PFA headquarters in Manchester. From there Gordon Taylor would carry it to Goodison Park for the surprise lunch.

Tension mounted until it was known that the USSR match would definitely be on.

Woodward sped up the M6 at 8.00 am on the Friday morning.

Disaster then struck: he hadn't realised the Queen was visiting Manchester that day. Because of this,

the traffic on the M6 had come to a
complete standstill.

Woodward was desperate. Why
hadn't everything been checked out?

There was no way of cutting through the traffic. As his fingers tapped the steering wheel Woodward knew that time was running out.

In the end he just made it, handing over the trophy to Gordon Taylor at about 12.10 am. Fortunately the Queen had left the city and Taylor reached Goodison Park in time.

Talking to the press about missing the dinner at the Grosvenor House Hotel, Lineker said, 'It was enough satisfaction to have won. I can't think of a better reason for missing the night than playing for England.'

Towards the end of that season, Lineker also received the Football Writers' Footballer of the Year

Award. This made him only the fourth player to win both awards in the same season.

■ CHAPTER FOUR

Soon after these triumphs, Lineker, playing in Mexico with England's 1986 World Cup Final squad, became the tournament's top scorer.

Because of this Lineker was head-hunted by Terry Venables of Spain's Barcelona for a fee of £4.2 million.

Once again, Lineker's tactics and long-term planning had paid off.

But he was not to remain long in Spain. After a row with the new manager, Johan Cruyff, Lineker returned to England, again head-hunted by Venables who was by now managing Tottenham.

He then helped Venables' team to win the FA Cup.

By 1991, Lineker was playing at the top of his form, but this was not to last and his international career ended when he was substituted by Graham Taylor during the 1992 European Championship in Sweden.

Bobby Robson, who took over as
manager of Barcelona from Johan
Cruyff, remembers that Lineker would
never pull out of a challenge. Once
the ball was in the box – he only saw

the ball. Nothing else! 'He went where the bullets fly, where some other players are afraid to go.' Robson never thought Lineker was a thrusting centre forward but relied on touch, timing and technique. 'He kept it simple and most of his goals were scored from inside the six-yard box. He was always looking for the space behind the defenders so that he could get in his shot.'

Lineker ended his career with an international goal total of 48 – only one goal short of the legendary Bobby Charlton.

After spending the final two years of his career playing for a Japanese club, Lineker became a different kind of star, presenting football programmes on TV.

Lineker's hard life of practice, self-criticism and practice again made him a brilliant example to anyone who felt they lacked natural talent but were determined to win.

Lineker said of his own game, 'As I progressed as a young player I began to think long and hard. I analysed my strengths – pace and an undeniable instinct for goals – and I worked on improving them.' Lineker also worked on his weaker points.

With that kind of thinking, Lineker is still an inspiration to many young would-be professional footballers today.

MATT BUSBY

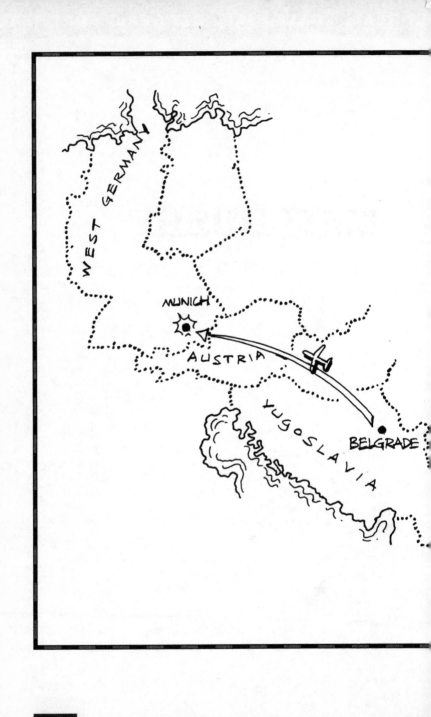

This map shows the first leg of the
Manchester United team's return from
Yugoslavia in 1958.

The aeroplane crash occurred at
Munich in southern Germany.

◼ CHAPTER ONE

Inside the plane's cabin, the
Manchester United team were
relaxing. It was February 6th, 1958,
and the plane was on the runway at
Munich airport.

The United manager, Matt Busby,
was very tired and wanted to get
home.

The day before, United had drawn
3-3 with the Red Star team in
Belgrade, Yugoslavia. This was the
second leg of the European Cup tie.

It saw United through to the semi-finals with a 5-4 aggregate.

After the match, a dinner had been given for both teams at the Majestic Hotel in Belgrade. Towards the end of the evening the lights were dimmed.

Waiters entered the room with burning candles and bowls of dessert. The whole of the United side clapped and the captain of the team sang *We'll Meet Again.*

Matt Busby then rose to his feet and said to the Red Star team and their guests, 'Come to us. The doors of Old Trafford will always be open to you.'

Forty-three passengers sat on the aeroplane that was still delayed at Munich airport. There were eight journalists and three club officials on board as well as the players.

Their plane had twice failed to get

off the runway due to the thick ice, slush and snow.

It had then taxied back to the terminal buildings for a check-up by the ground crew.

The passengers waited tensely in the airport lounge while this was being done.

■ CHAPTER TWO

A quarter of an hour later the passengers were back on board. The ground staff had said that all was well with the plane.

The time was 2.59 pm and a third take-off attempt was about to be made.

The last radio message from the control tower was the signal to start the engines. They got louder until they reached their familiar high-pitched whine.

The plane roared down the runway, picking up speed – 70 knots,

80 knots and then 117.

Peter Howard, a photographer from the *Daily Mail*, thought he heard the starboard engine note drop, rather like a car changing gear.

Frank Taylor, the *News Chronicle* sports writer, was on the other side of the plane and didn't hear the change in the engine noise. He was busy watching the port wheel and the huge amount of icy slush that was being thrown back as the plane roared on at high speed.

Shouldn't they be in the air by now? Taylor wondered. *Just how long was the runway?* They seemed to have been racing along for a very long time.

The plane had already passed the point on the runway where the stop had been made on the two failed take-offs. So why hadn't the port wheel gone up yet?

But most other passengers hadn't

noticed as they looked forward to the food and drink on the return flight.

'Has the wheel gone up yet?' Taylor shouted to Dennis Viollet, the Manchester United inside-left player.

There was no reply and Taylor reckoned Viollet couldn't hear his voice above the screaming of the engines.

Now Taylor couldn't be sure whether they had left the ground or not. The slush was like a haze outside the aircraft's windows.

Surely they must be in the air by now, Taylor thought. He knew he was

getting very upset and tried to calm
down. The pilots were in charge and
the plane had been checked by the
ground staff. They must know what
they were doing. Didn't they? So
what was he worrying about?

Then Taylor saw the fence that ran
around the airfield.

The aircraft seemed to be heading straight for it.

Taylor gasped in horror. All his worst fears were coming true. Some of the other passengers began to scream as they, too, saw the fence.

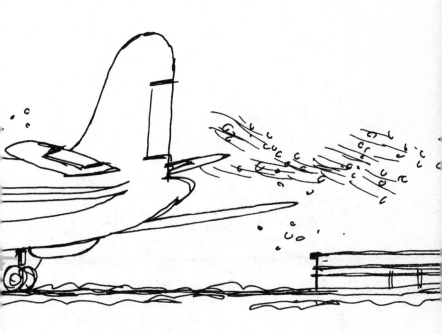

Then Taylor felt a hard blow behind his left arm and mercifully passed out as the aeroplane smashed through the fence. It crashed into a house and broke in two.

■ CHAPTER THREE

In England, no one could believe the terrible news. Earlier, the newspaper headlines had read *Manchester United Plane Held Up In Munich Snowstorm.*

As soon as news of the crash came through, the headlines were changed to *Manchester United Players in Plane Crash.*

On the streets crowds surrounded the news-stands. The BBC even broke into the long-running radio

soap opera of the time, *Mrs Dale's Diary*, to give the dreadful news.

Men and women, boys and girls wept openly in the streets.

Eight journalists, three club officials, two members of the air crew and eight United players were killed as well as two other passengers.

There were only twenty survivors.

Matt Busby had horrific injuries. His chest wall had been crushed, endangering his lungs. His right foot had been smashed. He was so ill that the news of the deaths was kept from him as he fought for his own life.

■ CHAPTER FOUR

Busby was rushed into hospital in Munich. His work as a football manager was in ruins. He could speak no German, but the doctors soon realised he was a man of great willpower.

He silently put up with acute physical pain and when it was felt he could be told about his dead friends, Busby took the grim news calmly. Inside his heart was broken.

Busby had lost Walter Crickmer, the Manchester United secretary,

Bert Whalley, United's coach, and Tom Curry, United's trainer. In addition, the young footballers who died were like sons to him and to lose them was a terrible blow.

Few people would have been able to survive such horrific physical and mental injuries, but Busby had a strong reason to want to live.

He was determined to rebuild the team.

This aim kept him going during the dark days in hospital. It was the only way he could cope with his grief. He would create a new team, a team that would win the European Cup for the UK. He owed that at least to his dead boys.

Later, Matt Busby was able to leave hospital and return home to England. There he watched Manchester United play against Bolton Wanderers in the Cup Final at Wembley.

Jimmy Murphy, who took over as manager while Busby was ill, had signed up new players.

Murphy, too, was determined that Manchester United should rise from the ashes of Munich.

He wrote in the United programme on February 19th, 1958:

'Although we mourn our dead and grieve for our wounded, we believe that great days are not done for us. The sympathy and encouragement of the football world and particularly of our supporters will justify and inspire us. The road back may be long and hard but with the memory of those who died at Munich ... Manchester United will rise again.'

Only a season earlier, the captain of Manchester United, Roger Byrne, had promised after being defeated by

Aston Villa, 'Never mind, we'll be back next year.'

Byrne was killed in the crash. But his words came true. Carried along on a high tide of emotion, Manchester United began to fight back. At first they had to use reserves and third-team players. But they seemed inspired.

The fifth round of the FA Cup had been put off to allow United time to form a new team. But in that fifth round they beat Sheffield Wednesday.

The next victory was against West Bromwich Albion when United beat

them 1-0 in the very last minute of a
replay. The spirit of Munich was once
again in the air. In the semi-final of
the FA Cup, a brilliant player named
Ernie Taylor joined United. He had
already gained cup winner medals
with Newcastle United and then later
with Blackpool as Stanley Matthews'
partner.

Crowther, the left half from Aston Villa, also joined United, and helped beat Fulham 5-3 in an exciting replay at Highbury after an opening 2-2 draw at Villa Park.

Amazingly, Manchester United were now on the last lap to Wembley and to winning the FA Cup.

The whole country wanted United to win, but the miracle couldn't continue. Two goals by Nat Lofthouse gave the trophy to Bolton Wanderers.

One of the most talented players killed at Munich was Duncan Edwards.

He had first played for United at the age of fifteen. At eighteen he was the youngest player to win an international cap.

Jimmy Murphy felt that Duncan Edwards was the one player who would have made rebuilding Manchester United so much easier – if only he had survived.

Matt Busby had trained Manchester United to be a brilliant team. After Munich, he set about building it up again. 'All I was hoping for was a reasonably safe place in the First Division until we got things sorted out,' he wrote. 'Those boys have played better than I dared hope. But a lot has to be done.'

A lot was done. Busby tried a new style of football. Instead of relying on fitness and speed, he expected his players to use their minds. Tactics became more important than just physical strength. The new technique paid off. In 1961 Manchester United won the League and Cup double. In 1963 they won the European Cup Winners' Cup.

Busby was triumphant as he watched his team from the touchline.

He had carried on the magic. Maybe that was because the spirit of the dead players had become so much part of him.

ERIC CANTONA

CHAPTER ONE

Cantona was having a rough ride.

It was 1995 and Manchester United were hopeful they were going to come top in the League Championship. If they won, this would be their third win in a row. But they were in a race against Blackburn Rovers and at the moment the teams were neck and neck.

On Wednesday January 25th, Manchester United were in second place. If they could beat Crystal

Palace at Selhurst Park, they
would win.

In fact, the result was 1-1 and a
great disappointment. But it wasn't
the disappointment that made the
headlines.

Eric Cantona had become involved
in a fight with a spectator. When the
incident had been fully looked into,
the public realised that football
players were coming under more and
more pressure. They were seen as
super-heroes by their fans who felt let
down by a team failure or even one
player's poor performance. No one
could have an off-day, and it wasn't
just the fans who made the protests.
There were the managers, the board,

the football writers, the transfer fees
– all big stress factors to any player.

Cantona was a brilliant Frenchman
who played for Manchester United.
He had only been in England for
twenty-six months when he became
the Football Association's Player of
the Year.

Cantona was born in Paris on May
24th, 1966. He played centre forward
and there could be no doubt that he
was a great footballer. He had
amazing control of the ball and many
footballing tricks, all of which he had
worked out for himself.

Cantona was very cool and laid back. His shirt collar was always casually turned up and his face showed no interest in what was going on around him. That, of course, was misleading; in fact he was totally focused. He was a good actor and could fool many opposing players.

■ CHAPTER TWO

But Cantona's arrogance often annoyed his critics as well as doing a great deal to break his opponents' self-confidence.

When Cantona came to England he already had a very fiery history with the French clubs he had played for.

His temper seemed to have snapped time and time again. Cantona might have brilliant ball control but he seemed to have little self-control, and in France there had usually been at least one incident per season.

In 1987 he was fined for hitting his own goalkeeper.

In 1988, Cantona insulted football coach Henri Michel while playing for the French national side. As a result he was banned.

In 1989, Cantona was suspended for kicking the ball into a stand and throwing his shirt at the referee.

In 1990, Cantona was banned for ten days after a clash with a team mate.

In 1991, he threw a ball at a referee. Later, Cantona lost his temper at the disciplinary hearing.

In 1992, he disappeared after walking out on the French club, Nîmes.

All this was quite a record – but it was also a record that turned Cantona into a legend.

The English fans were curious, for Cantona made any match that he played in both exciting and tense. No one ever knew what he was going to do next. Possibly, neither did Cantona.

His temper could break out without warning. But so could his displays of great football. He gave the side he was playing for an extra edge and worried the opposition.

■ CHAPTER THREE

After he walked out on Nîmes, Cantona crossed the Channel and turned up at Hillsborough.

It was announced that he was going to play for Sheffield Wednesday, then trying to become one of the top three teams in the First Division.

Trevor Francis, the manager, said that Eric Cantona should have a week's trial. Then he could take a careful look at the French player's skills.

Self-confident as ever, Cantona told
the press, 'A player like me does not
need testing.'

Francis was concerned. Surely
testing was fair. He had to see for
himself if Cantona was really as good
as he was said to be.

Angry that he was being judged, Cantona joined Leeds United instead, and played fifteen games before the season came to an end. This earned him a championship medal when Leeds beat Manchester United in the FA Cup final. Leeds United had proved Cantona didn't need testing – at least as far as skilful play was concerned.

In November 1992, after a further thirteen matches for Leeds in the new Premier League, Cantona told the press that he was going to leave Leeds. He was upset that he was not getting a first-team place all the time. Once again his need to be praised and praised again was not being fulfilled – in his eyes anyway.

Cantona was a brilliant player, but he always had to be treated as a superstar.

He took a risk by leaving Leeds, but his face was saved by Manchester United who offered £1.2 million to bring him to Old Trafford. Now Cantona was really pleased. At last he was being seen as the great player he knew he was.

■ CHAPTER FOUR

Cantona appeared in twenty-two games before the end of the season. He ended up top scorer with nine goals to his credit.

Manchester United won the 1992-93 Premiership title. They were ten points ahead of Aston Villa. Cantona became the first player to win for two years in a row but playing for two different clubs. Cantona had shown he really was a superstar.

His legend grew and his play continued to improve. Fans always looked forward to his dazzling appearances and he seemed to command the ball like a magician.

But with Cantona's brilliance came his temper, and Manchester United's continued success in 1993-94 was marred by a problem with Cantona in the European Cup. His temper seemed to be getting on top of him.

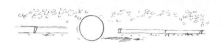

Despite this, everyone agreed that he was by far the best United player that season.

Cantona then won the Player of the Year award. When he was given the trophy, he said, 'I would like to thank other people from football in England, even the player who did not vote for me.'

But Cantona's good humour wasn't to last. In March he was suspended after two sendings-off in four days.

As a result he missed Manchester United's match against Oldham Athletic in the FA Cup semi-final at Wembley. He also missed the replay.

Cantona returned for the last five games of the League. He became the club's top scorer with a total of 18 goals. Two of these were kicked in from the penalty spot.

Cantona also played in the FA Cup final against Chelsea on May 14th, 1994. Displaying all his skills, he scored two goals, helping United to win 4-0.

Despite all the problems, there could be no doubt that Cantona played each game with his heart and soul. Sadly, the pressure was often too much for him.

In 1995 Manchester United were playing a tense game against Crystal Palace at Selhurst Park. Early in the second half a tackle from Richard Shaw had caught Cantona from behind. A little later, when Cantona and Shaw challenged each other for a high clearance from another Crystal Palace player, Cantona lost his temper.

As a result he was sent off by the referee for the fifth time in sixteen months.

Cantona walked towards the touch-line, feeling publicly put down. His anger was not just with the referee but with the crowd itself.

Football is not a game that can always be played in a laid-back way. The great pressure on the players makes many of them crack up. This time it was Cantona's turn, and a fuse was lit to an extra-large rocket.

As Eric Cantona walked sadly back to his dressing room, one of the spectators ran forward, shouting abuse and gesturing at him.

With a flash of temper, Cantona leapt across the barrier and the two men fought. The stewards and the police had to get between them.

This time Cantona had gone too far.

Manchester United not only fined him two weeks' wages but suspended him for the rest of the season.

An FA enquiry into the incident suspended Cantona until the following October.

The French FA then stripped him of the captaincy of the national side.

Eric Cantona now faced his worst crisis ever. He was known to be hot-tempered and his temper had always been part of his legend. This time, despite all his talents, the footballing authorities were forced to punish him. No one, however skilled, can get away with giving the game a bad name for violence.

Over the years, many spectators have often behaved badly. Fans are often seen as little better than hooligans. Players can't afford to be seen as hooligans too.

Despite this, Eric Cantona's reputation as a brilliant player has already ensured him a place in football history.

GLOSSARY

aggregate the collective number of goals scored.

Division (Premiership, First, Second, Third) groups into which the teams are divided according to the results of the previous year.

FA Cup Final the final game that decides which team wins the Football Association Cup Trophy for the year.

hat trick three goals scored by one player during a game.

haze mist.

Hillsborough Sheffield Wednesday's home football ground.

hooligans thugs who start fights.

League Championship the competition comprised of Divisions. Points are awarded to teams who win or draw. At the end of the season the team with the most points wins the League. The teams who do best are promoted to a higher Division, and the teams who do worst are relegated to a lower Division.

Old Trafford Manchester United's home football ground.

penalty a free kick given as a result of a breach of rules by the opposing side.

PFA Professional Football Association.

port left-hand side of an aircraft or ship.

professional someone who is paid to play a game.

replay a match held for the second time because the two teams were equal in the first match.

reserves players who are ready to play if needed.

scout someone who looks out for good players.

slush melting snow.

starboard right-hand side of an aircraft or ship.

strike partners players who help each other to score goals.

striker a player who scores goals.

suspended not allowed to play.

tackle an attempt to take the ball away from an opposing player.

tactics plan of how to achieve the best results.

tournament a series of games to find an overall winner.

transfer fees money paid to a club to buy one of their players.

USSR Union of Soviet Socialist Republics. Formerly known as the Soviet Bloc, or the union of Communist countries. Now all these countries are independent.

Daring Escapes

*Luis knew the main battle was raging in the valley
and it would be crazy to go down there.
The bullets thudded around the rocks.
Luis realised he could be hit at any moment.*

*Read Daring Escapes and find out how ordinary
people cheated death in wartime.*

Mountain Horror

Jon had to get himself going. He had to make decisions. Above all he needed a plan. If he slipped off the icy slope he would die at once. But that would be better than dying slowly on the mountain.

Read Mountain Horror and find out how climbers survived against all the odds.

Terror at Sea

*Jacques and Frédéric thought they might be able
to escape – that is, unless one of them got wounded.
At the first sign of blood the sharks
would attack them both.*

*Read Terror at Sea and find out about narrow escapes
from a watery grave.*